INSIGHT GUIDES

COLORADO

Discovery CHANNEL

APA PUBLICATIONS
Part of the Langenscheidt Publishing Group

INSIGHT GUIDE
COLORADO

ABOUT THIS BOOK

Editorial
Editor
John Gattuso
Editorial Director
Brian Bell

Distribution

United States
Langenscheidt Publishers, Inc.
46–35 54th Road, Maspeth, NY 11378
Fax: 1 (718) 784 0640

Canada
Thomas Allen & Son Ltd
390 Steelcase Road East
Markham, Ontario L3R 1G2
Fax: (1) 905 475 6747

UK & Ireland
GeoCenter International Ltd
The Viables Centre, Harrow Way
Basingstoke, Hants RG22 4BJ
Fax: (44) 1256 817988

Australia
Universal Publishers
1 Waterloo Road
Macquarie Park, NSW 2113
Fax: (61) 2 9888 9074

New Zealand
Hema Maps New Zealand Ltd (HNZ)
Unit D, 24 Ra ORA Drive
East Tamaki, Auckland
Fax: (64) 9 273 6479

Worldwide
**Apa Publications GmbH & Co.
Verlag KG (Singapore branch)**
38 Joo Koon Road, Singapore 628990
Tel: (65) 6865 1600. Fax: (65) 6861 6438

Printing

Insight Print Services (Pte) Ltd
38 Joo Koon Road, Singapore 628990
Tel: (65) 6865 1600. Fax: (65) 6861 6438

©2004 Apa Publications GmbH & Co.
Verlag KG (Singapore branch)
All Rights Reserved

First Edition 2004

This guidebook combines the
interests and enthusiasms of
two of the world's best known information providers: Insight Guides,
whose titles have set the standard
for visual travel guides since 1970,
and Discovery Channel, the world's
premier source of nonfiction televi-
sion programming.

The editors of Insight Guides provide practical advice and general
understanding about a destination's
history, culture, natural resources,
institutions and people. Discovery
Channel and its Web site, www.dis-
covery.com, help millions of viewers
explore their world from the comfort
of their own homes and encourage
them to explore it firsthand.

Insight Guide: Colorado is struc-
tured to convey an understanding of
the state and its people as well as
to guide readers through its sights:

◆ The **Features** section, indicated
by a yellow bar at the top of each
page, covers the natural and cultural
history of the state in a series of
informative essays.

◆ The main **Places** section, indicated by a blue bar, is a complete
guide to all the sights and areas
worth visiting. Places of special
interest are coordinated by number
with the maps.

◆ The **Travel Tips** listings section,
with an orange bar, provides full
information on travel, hotels, shops,
restaurants and more. An easy-to-
find contents list for Travel Tips is
printed on the back flap, which also
serves as a bookmark.

The contributors

This book was produced by **John Gattuso** of Stone Creek Publications in
Milford, New Jersey, a veteran of

ABOVE: "dudes" on a trail ride at the Saddleback Ranch, Milner, Colorado.

more than a dozen Insight Guides and editor of the Discovery Travel Adventures, a series for travelers with special interests.

Santa Fe writer **Nicky Leach** has worked with John for more than 10 years, creating Insight Guides on the American West. She jumped at the chance to revisit neighboring Colorado, handling chapters on Mesa Verde, the Northwest Corner and the San Juan Mountains. Her favorite destination? Echo Canyon in Dinosaur National Monument, one of the most spectacular but least-known places in the National Park System. Nicky also wrote about Colorado's natural history and ancient cultures.

Richard Harris, a native Colo-

radan, is the author or co-author of more than 30 guidebooks on the American West, Mexico and Central America. In this book, he gives an overview of Colorado's "Cultural Landscape" as well as covering the I-70 corridor west of Denver and the Aspen region. When not traveling, he lives in Santa Fe, where he is president of the New Mexico Book Association and publisher of *Southwest BookViews*.

Claire Walter is an award-winning author of hundreds of magazine articles and many books. A resident of Colorado since 1988, she specializes in writing about the great outdoors. In this book, she shares her expertise on skiing, adventure and Colorado cuisine as well as covering Boulder and Steamboat Springs.

Conger Beasley didn't have to stray too far from home to do the research for this book. The Colorado Springs writer covered his hometown as well as the San Luis Valley and vast eastern plains. He is the author of more than a dozen books, including a guide to the national parks of the Rocky Mountains.

With more than 30 years experience as a news editor in the New York area, **Edward A. Jardim** knows how to transform a complex story into a concise narrative. Here he condenses three centuries of history into an engaging chronicle of Colorado's development, from pioneering expeditions like those of Zebulon Pike and John Frémont to the growth of vibrant cities like Denver and Colorado Springs.

Richard Nowitz, a regular contributor to Insight Guides, was the principal photographer. The book was indexed by **Elizabeth Cook;** the map editor was **Zoë Goodwin**.

Map Legend

– – – –	State Boundary
– ▪ – ▪ –	National Park/Reserve
✈ ✦	Airport: International/Regional
🚌	Bus Station
❶	Tourist Information
✉	Post Office
🏛 † ✝	Church/Ruins
†	Monastery
☾	Mosque
✡	Synagogue
🏰 🏯	Castle/Ruins
🏠	Mansion/Stately home
∴	Archeological Site
∩	Cave
𝟏	Statue/Monument
★	Place of Interest

The main places of interest in the Places section are coordinated by number with a full-color map (e.g. ❶), and a symbol at the top of every right-hand page tells you where to find the map.

INSIGHT GUIDE
COLORADO

CONTENTS

Maps

Introduction

History

Features

A waterfall tumbles down a mountainside in Rocky Mountain National Park.

Travel Tips

Information panels

Places

ROCKY MOUNTAIN STATE

*Soaring peaks, world-class skiing and vibrant cities
lure travelers to America's alpine heartland*

"The scenery bankrupts the English language," said Theodore Roosevelt, a man rarely at a loss for words. TR was musing about the Rocky Mountains during a visit to Colorado in 1901. The landscape will do that to people. Words fail to capture the skyward sweep of it all, the heady mix of humility and exaltation one feels standing atop its legendary peaks, 54 of them soaring beyond 14,000 ft (4,270 meters).

Of course, modern man has made his mark here, too. Roads blasted from the bedrock appear to curve right up to the heavens. Railroads twist and turn, like corkscrews, up impossibly steep terrain. Dams block the course of rivers. Bridges and tunnels span what appear to be insurmountable distances. And is any feat of modern engineering equivalent in daring to the ancient cliff dwellings of Mesa Verde, laid up stone by stone in narrow canyon alcoves by people who somehow got by without wheelbarrows, pulleys or levels?

Still, we're reminded how brief and transitory it can all be. Once upon a time, mining towns extracted huge yields of gold and silver from deep within the earth. Now, in most cases, they are little more than ruins. The wind rattles, ghost-like, through tumble-down saloons, cabins and headframes.

Eroding from the ground elsewhere in Colorado are bones of creatures – Diplodocus, Stegosaurus, Camarasaurus – who trod the planet long before our earliest apelike ancestors made their debut. Colorado has produced more dinosaur fossils than any other state in the Union, and it is a veritable trove of dinosaur trackways – footprints left on the shore of an ancient sea and now embedded forever in solid rock, like a message from a distant world.

And then there are the Rockies, backbone of the continent. At 30 million years old, they are approaching middle age, though their peaks, carved by glacial ice into "cirques," "hanging valleys" and knife-edged "aretes," retain the assertive thrust of youth.

Even on the eastern plains, where grasslands roll gently to the horizon, one feels a bit subdued by the landscape. Out on the prairie, there's both an oceanic sense of space and a personal feeling of smallness, as if you're no more than a cork bobbing on the waves.

Land and landscape – Colorado's heart and soul. Yes, there are vibrant cities, charming towns, art and culture, great restaurants, rafting, hiking, some of the world's best skiing, and much else. But behind it all, always, is the land itself. That is the essence of Colorado, the magic it shares with every visitor. ❑

PRECEDING PAGES: a climber surveys the scene from Longs Peak; kayaking the Animas River; a hiker rests at Blue Lake Pass in the San Juan Mountains.
LEFT: Indian paintbrush blooms in the Snefels Wilderness.

Decisive Dates

Early cultures

circa **11,000 BC:** Paleo-Indians inhabit the region that includes present-day Colorado.

AD 1: Ancient Puebloans emerge in the Four Corners region.

circa **1300:** A severe drought forces inhabitants of the Mesa Verde region to abandon complex pueblo communities.

circa **1500:** On the eve of Spanish entry, Colorado is inhabited chiefly by Arapaho and Cheyenne in the eastern Plains and by Ute in the west.

Strangers from afar

1541: Returning from his trailblazing expedition in search of the mythical Seven Cities of Cíbola, Francisco Vásquez de Coronado probably crosses the southeastern corner of Colorado.

1682: The region east of the Rockies is claimed for France by explorer La Salle.

1706: An expedition of Spaniards and Indians under Juan de Uribarri visits Apache villages near present-day Pueblo.

1739: A group of Frenchmen led by the trade-minded Mallet brothers passes through eastern Colorado en route to Santa Fe in New Mexico.

1765: As the first European prospectors in Colorado, Juan Maria de Rivera and his fellow Spaniards explore the San Juan and Sangre de Cristo Ranges.

1779: In a battle south of the Arkansas River, a Spanish force under Juan Bautista de Anza defeats a Comanche force headed by Cuerno Verde.

Americans move in

1803: Most of present-day eastern Colorado becomes an American possession through the Louisiana Purchase.

1806: The first American to formally explore the Colorado area is Lt. Zebulon M. Pike, who with a party of 22 men pushes into the mountains west of Pueblo and Colorado Springs.

1820: An exploratory mission is conducted by an Army force commanded by Maj. Stephen H. Long.

1832: At the height of the "mountain man" era, Bent's Fort is built by the Bents and St. Vrain Company near the present city of La Junta.

1842: The first of five exploratory missions that involve the Rocky Mountain region is conducted by Lt. John C. Frémont.

1846: En route to his conquest of New Mexico, Gen. Stephen W. Kearney leads his "Army of the West" over the Santa Fe Trail through southeastern Colorado. Two years later, Mexico cedes to the United States most of western Colorado.

1851: First permanent settlement in Colorado founded at Conejos in the San Luis Valley by six Hispanic families. Meanwhile, the Treaty of Fort Laramie assures the Cheyenne and Arapaho tribes all of Colorado's eastern plain.

1853: Capt. John W. Gunnison leads an exploring party across southern and western Colorado. Weeks later, he is killed by Paiute Indians in Utah.

Boom times

1858: Small deposits of gold are found near the South Platte River and Cherry Creek, kicking off Colorado's gold rush. Denver City is founded.

1859: John Gregory's gold strike at North Clear Creek on May 6 overcomes wavering belief in the territory's mining prospects. As many as 40,000 gold-diggers flock to Colorado.

1861: Congress establishes the Colorado Territory. Population: 25,371.

1863: Denver's central area is destroyed by fire. Cherry Creek floods the following year.

1864: Cavalrymen slaughter about 150 Cheyenne and Arapaho at Sand Creek.

1867: Under the Treaty of Medicine Lodge, members of the Cheyenne and Arapaho tribes agree to move to reservations in Oklahoma. Denver becomes the territorial capital.

1871: Colorado Springs is founded by Gen. William J. Palmer.

1875: Rich silver deposits are found near Leadville.

1876: Colorado is admitted to the Union.

1879: Indian agent Nathan C. Meeker is slain along with several others in a Ute uprising.

1881: Ute tribes are removed onto reservations.

1888: Two cowboys discover the ancient ruins of Cliff Palace at Mesa Verde.

1891: One of the world's great gold strikes is made at Cripple Creek. Gold production reaches a peak of more than $20 million annually by 1900.

1893: Colorado becomes the second state in the Union to grant women full voting rights.

killed during the Ludlow Massacre, pitting miners against state militia near Trinidad.

1915: Rocky Mountain National Park created.

1917: "Buffalo Bill" Cody dies and is buried on Lookout Mountain west of Denver.

1918: World War I stimulates molybdenum mining; coal output reaches a new high of 12 million tons.

1931: The state's population exceeds one million.

1946: Uranium discovered near Grand Junction.

1950s: Colorado's population climbs steadily, as does its reputation as a recreation haven.

1958: The Air Force Academy opens.

1959: The Colorado-Big Thompson system brings water to the state's populous eastern region.

1893: Congress repeals the Sherman Silver Purchase Act, wreaking havoc on the silver industry.

A new century

1903–04: Miners strike for better working conditions. Militia are summoned to break strikes by the Western Federation of Miners.

1905–06: At least 113 Coloradans die in snow avalanches, 22 at a single mine near Silverton.

1914: Twenty people, including 12 children, are

PRECEDING PAGES: a buggy creeps along the Otto Mears toll road near Bear Creek Falls, 1909.

LEFT: ancient cliff dwelling, Mesa Verde National Park.

ABOVE: Cripple Creek Railroad, *circa* 1900.

1974: Huge deposits of shale oil are tapped on the Western Slope, setting off another boom.

1976: Coloradans worried about mushrooming growth vote against hosting the Winter Olympics.

1982: Exxon closes oil fields in western Colorado. The 1980s bring growth in the high-tech sector.

1992: Voters approve a state constitutional amendment to circumscribe privileges for homosexuals; the "Anti-Gay Initiative" is invalidated by the Colorado Supreme Court.

1993: The Colorado Rockies take to the field in Denver for the state's first major-league baseball game.

1995: Denver International Airport opens.

2000: Colorado's population reaches 4,301,261, an increase of over 1 million in just a decade. ❑

NATIVE HERITAGE

For countless generations, the people of this land hunted
and farmed and fashioned intricate ways of dealing with nature

This land was their land, once upon a time. The first people to move into this place called Colorado seem to have arrived from Asia some 12,000 years ago, at the tail end of the Ice Age. Crossing into Alaska via the exposed land mass known as Beringia, they followed big game inland, down to where the Eastern Rockies meet the Great Plains.

They found a landscape of peaks and plains and cool mountain streams capable of nourishing all living things. The hunting was good – herds of giant bison, camel, horse, elk, deer and antelope, clustered around lakes and marshes that also held 7-ft-long (2-meter) beavers and giant ground sloths. But the big prize was mammoths. Hunters pursued the huge, tusked creatures along the eastern Rockies, sleeping in cave shelters and flaking stone spear points around campfires. They butchered on site, leaving behind bones, chipped stone and chert spear points of a type known as Clovis, for the town in New Mexico where they were first identified.

By 9000 BC, climatic warming and possibly overhunting had doomed many of the large animals. Paleoindians focused instead on one creature – the giant bison. Big-game hunting required bravery and cooperation, skills that would later characterize the tribes that wandered the Plains in search of bison in the historic period. They knapped smaller spear points from obsidian obtained from high-country sites like Black Mountain near the headwaters of the Rio Grande in the San Juans. The Folsom, as they came to be called, were widespread throughout Colorado. Campsites have been found on the Wyoming border, near Fort Collins, and in the San Luis Valley. Anywhere, in fact, where there was grass and water to support huge herds of bison.

A thousand years later, people of the Plano culture had refined bison hunting to a fine art, cleverly killing large numbers by herding them over cliffs. Some 200 bison were found at the

Olsen Chabbuck "buffalo jump" in southeastern Colorado. Eventually, the giant bison, too, vanished, supplanted by modern bison of a much smaller size. And once again humans adapted, not only embracing the changing environment but becoming expert in the great variety of plants and animals to be found there.

Man and nature

The long-running Archaic period may well have been the most successful in human history. Small bands wandered large, defined territories, stopping at favored campsites to hunt and harvest seasonally. It was a lifestyle that sustained the Utes of western Colorado for centuries – a perfect balance of man and nature.

Archaic people camped near springs, streams and rivers throughout Colorado, making use of rock shelters and portable hide tents known as wickiups. They hunted year-round, using snares and traps to capture small animals such as prairie dogs, rabbits and squirrels, and an atlatl, or spear-thrower, to bring down bison, deer,

LEFT: grinding stones at Step House, Mesa Verde National Park.
RIGHT: Ute Indian rock art, Mancos Canyon.

antelope, bighorn sheep and elk. In summer, they gathered prairie turnips, wild mustard, buffalo berries and plums on the plains and harvested sweet, nutritious pinyon nuts from higher elevations. These wild plants were placed in woven baskets attached to a tumpline and strapped around the forehead of women, who also carried babies this way.

A warming trend between 7,500 and 4,500 years ago, known as the Altithermal, may have encouraged some Archaic people to move to the Uncompahgre Plateau, where greater moisture supported more plants and animals. A number of sites, including some now immersed

pithouses as early as 6,000 years ago. One 3,000-year-old pithouse was excavated east of Grand Junction. At this unusual site, archaeologists uncovered a variety of wild ricegrass that had been cultivated to produce large seeds. By AD 100, the idea of growing food had also reached hunter-gatherers in the eastern Rockies, who were in contact with agricultural cultures in the Ohio Valley, from whom they learned home building and pottery made with a paddle and anvil.

Pueblo farmers

The tribes who lived along the Republican, Apishpa, Purgatoire, Arkansas and South Platte

under Curecanti Reservoir in the Gunnison River Valley, appear to date from this time. By 2000 BC, hunters were leaving split-twig fetishes of bighorn sheep in high cliffs where the sheep often traveled, hoping to attract the real thing perhaps. Shamans may also have undertaken long pilgrimages to sacred sites and prayed for help. Camped beneath sheer sandstone cliffs, they painted images in red hematite on the walls: herds of bighorn sheep, flowing water and lifesize, triangular figures with long thin bodies and huge, empty eyes that hovered wraithlike above dry sandy washes.

Archaic people were living in semicircular, underground homes with earthen roofs known as

Rivers remained hunter-gatherers until pressure from incoming tribes and European settlers doomed their way of life in the 1800s. But the Basketmakers who lived in the canyon country of the Four Corners eagerly embraced farming.

Mexican corn culture, pottery making and building stone pueblos reached the Four Corners via traders from the south early in the Christian era. From the Hohokam, who practiced irrigation farming in southern Arizona, the Basketmakers may have acquired exotic goods from Mexico and learned how to use check dams, ditches and dry farming techniques. From the Mogollon of southern New Mexico, they learned how to make pots using the coiled clay method and to fire them at high temperatures to make strong, airtight containers for storing and transporting grain. The refined pottery of the Four Corners quickly became a sought-after trade item.

By the early Pueblo I period (AD 700–900), extended families throughout the Four Corners were living in hamlets of above-ground houses made of sandstone and adobe. Pithouses were used as underground ceremonial rooms, or kivas. Here clansmen gathered to weave cotton and discuss the most advantageous times to plant and harvest. Ritual specialists tracked the daily movements of the sun, moon and planets across the sky. As the solstices approached, ceremonies were announced, and the priests quickly became the most important members of the village.

The Fremont

The people who lived in northwestern Colorado had much in common with their neighbors to the south. They too made pottery, grew corn, squash and later beans, and lived together in villages. But for them the hunter-gatherer lifestyle of their Archaic ancestors still beckoned. The Fremont are less obvious in the archaeological record, perhaps because of their fondness for remote places. They developed a hardy strain of corn that suited the highlands, fashioned plain, utilitarian pottery, and made moccasins with the dew claw of a deer for traction.

Long after the Anasazi, or Ancestral Pueblo, of the Four Corners were building large stone villages, the Fremont found comfort in pithouses – by far, the most practical shelter in the cold winters and warm summers of the high desert. Their rock art, too, echoed that of early Archaic people, with depictions of large-shouldered anthropomorphs and game animals and enigmatic figures like Kokopelli, the flute player. Hundreds of Fremont pictographs dot the Douglas Creek drainage, between Grand Junction and Rangely. More can be found throughout Dinosaur National Monument, in Echo Canyon and along the Green River near Dinosaur Quarry.

The Chaco phenomenon

By the Pueblo II period (AD 900–1100), the Southwest was dominated by one major Pueblo group: the powerful Chaco civilization, centered on Chaco Canyon, New Mexico. Archaeologists speculate that Chaco may have served as a sort of Vatican City for people living in the San Juan Basin, just south of southwestern Colorado. Seasonal ceremonies at Chaco, and redistribution of trade goods from as far away as the Pacific, the Mississippi River and Mexico may have brought thousands to the remote canyon.

Satellite villages, or outliers, such as the Escalante Ruin at Anasazi Heritage Center, north of Cortez, and Chimney Rock, east of Durango, seem to have played roles in the Chaco system. Both served as pioneer Chaco communities in

outlying areas, housed in typical Chaco pueblos with several kivas. The two distinctive rock formations at Chimney Rock seem to have been used by an isolated community of men living nearby. They apparently tracked the moon and cut high-country pines, which were floated down the Piedras River to Chaco for construction.

The Chaco culture crashed spectacularly in the early 1100s. Its leaders may have become straw men in the face of long-running drought, leaving desperate farming families to their own devices. They fled to surrounding highlands, where resources were more plentiful, and clashed with existing residents. By the early Pueblo III period (AD 1100–1300), the

LEFT: Fremont Culture pictographs known as the "Carrot Men" adorn Book Cliffs in western Colorado.
RIGHT: a reconstructed Basketmaker pithouse.

Montezuma Valley of southwestern Colorado had an estimated population of 30,000. Villages sprang up on every mesa with a stream. Lookout towers were built, perhaps to safeguard communities from outsiders.

These enclosed pueblos were hastily constructed, using large stones loosely mortared with mud, and some were now built in unusual shapes, such as the oval, circular, square and "D" shaped buildings at Hovenweep National Monument.

Inside warm, south-facing canyon walls, next to springs, they built some 600 cliff dwellings, ranging from small villages to major ceremonial centers, such as Cliff Palace, whose unusual tower kiva was probably used for astronomical observations. These cliff dwellings represented the last phase of Ancestral Pueblo life in the Four Corners. By 1300, the region was abandoned. Families moved south to New Mexico and Arizona to live along more reliable lands next to the Rio Grande and

> **FOOD FOR THOUGHT**
>
> Did the Ancient Puebloans engage in cannibalism? Archaeologist Christy Turner thinks so. He argues that Aztecs from Mexico used human sacrifice to subjugate Puebloans, a theory supported by the discovery of fossilized feces containing human remains.

Mesa Verde

Just east of modern-day Cortez, Mesa Verde, an 8,517-ft-high (2,596-meter) plateau with warm southern exposures and stream-carved finger canyons, had been a popular farming spot for generations. When white settlers explored it in the late 1800s, they found more than 4,000 sites, from early pithouses and small pueblos to extensive fields and an unfinished, 12th-century ceremonial center on Chapin Mesa. Thousands of bowls, effigy pots, mugs, ladles and other black-on-white pottery lay among the ruins.

Beginning in the late 1100s and 1200s, residents of Mesa Verde left their mesa-top villages and moved into homes concealed in the cliffs.

Little Colorado River. The inhabitants of 24 modern pueblos trace their ancestry to Mesa Verde.

At its height, Mesa Verde supported 5,000 people. By the end of the Great Drought of 1276–1300, Mesa Verde and the surrounding Montezuma Valley could no longer support the population. Without rain, fields didn't produce and wild foods disappeared. There must have been competition for what little remained. Violent episodes became more frequent.

The arrival of newcomers may have tipped the balance. Intriguing new evidence suggests that nomadic Athabascans from northwest Canada, who split into the Navajo and Apache tribes in the Southwest, were already in the area by the late 12th century. Utes from the Great Basin may have arrived soon after. These tribes vied for dominance in the areas abandoned by Ancestral Pueblo and Fremont farmers.

Plains culture

Just as farming transformed the lives of Pueblo people, horses revolutionized the lives of buffalo hunters on the Plains. Introduced by the Spanish in the late 17th century, horses were able to draw heavily laden sleds, or *travois*, from place to place. Men on horseback joined other groups to hunt bison over larger areas. They left for long periods, leaving behind their families to gather

vision quests fasted on mountain tops, seeking spiritual guidance. Most tribes practiced the Sun Dance, in which men fasted, danced, and pierced their flesh with hooks tied to a central pole – a sacrifice intended to benefit the whole tribe.

The first tribe to acquire horses in Colorado was probably the Ute, whose people were widespread throughout Colorado in the 1600s. They fought the Navajo and eventually forced them to retreat into New Mexico and Arizona. In 1700, the Jicarilla Apaches in southeastern Colorado and Kansas were pushed into New Mexico by advancing Comanches from the north, armed with French guns. By 1775, the

food, tan bison skins, and make clothing at encampments of hide-covered tents, or tipis.

A man's wealth was now counted by the number of horses he owned, and his success in hunting bison and raiding other tribes for horses and slaves was vital to his status as a warrior. Warrior societies, such as the feared Cheyenne Dog Soldiers, grew up in Plains tribes, whose members performed feats of bravery during battle, such as touching their enemies (counting coup) and collecting scalps. Young men on

ABOVE: Cliff Palace, which was abandoned in the late 13th century, is the largest cliff dwelling in North America, with more than 215 rooms and 23 kivas.

Comanche found themselves pushed south of the Arkansas River by Kiowa and Kiowa-Apaches. An alliance of Comanches, Kiowas and Kiowa-Apaches dominated the Southern Plains and inspired fear in the Pueblos of the Rio Grande as well as European settlers.

In the early 1800s, Arapahos displaced from the Great Lakes took up bison hunting on the Plains. They wandered the eastern Rockies, camping seasonally in favorite spots in the Denver area and, along with Cheyenne and Sioux allies, raided Crows, Shoshones, Utes, Comanches and others.

French and American fur trappers now appeared in Colorado. In the 1830s, mountain man rendezvous took place at Fort Davy Crockett in Browns Park and Bent's Fort on the Arkansas River, where beads, blankets, kettles, knives, whiskey and guns were bartered for beaver pelts and buffalo hides, along with prized deerskin clothing made by Ute women.

Relations between traders and Indians were generally peaceful and resulted in important alliances. Trader William Bent married a Cheyenne woman. Their eastern-educated son George would survive the bloody Sand Creek Massacre of 1864 and provide an important eyewitness account of the atrocity. Another trader married a young Arapaho woman who taught English to her brother Niwot, or Left Hand. The multilingual Niwot became a highly respected leader dedicated to peaceful coexistence during the Indian Wars. It was near Bent's Fort, in 1840, that the Southern Arapaho and Cheyenne made permanent peace with the Kiowa and Comanche, following the devastating Battle of Wolf Creek in 1837.

Manifest Destiny

After Mexico ceded much of the Southwest to the United States in 1848, white-Indian relations grew increasingly strained. Over the next decade, gold was discovered in both Califor-

NEUTRAL GROUND

No trip to Bent's Fort is complete without a stroll through the bosque shading the banks of the Arkansas River. It's pleasant to walk there, through tall grass edging the steep banks, past stands of willow and box elder, listening to cottonwood leaves fluttering overhead. A flat stem enables the leaves to turn 180 degrees in a slight breeze. In the days before air conditioning, people sat under the trees to enjoy the extra breath stirred up by the shivering leaves. The wind makes a distinctive sound as it soughs through these gnarly old trees with their stout trunks, splintered branches, and runneled bark.

It's easy to imagine hundreds of tipis pitched alongside the path of the river. William Bent reported that in the spring of 1842 thousands of Indians from half a dozen tribes were camped up and down the Arkansas within view of the fort. Bent's Fort was neutral ground, and all animosities, tribal and personal, were suspended for as long as the tribes were camped there.

The Indians engaged in horse races, powwows, religious ceremonies and long trading sessions with the factors at the fort. Young men used this lull in their normal lives to court young women, and at night the reedy tremolo of love flutes could be heard over the barking of dogs and the whinnying of horses.

nia and Colorado. Huge numbers of miners and settlers headed west on the Santa Fe and Oregon Trails to seek their fortunes. They destroyed favorite Indian campsites with their cattle and homesteads and slaughtered buffalo by the millions, mostly for sport. Government policies instigated private ownership of what had once been communal lands, and Indians were deprived of their livelihoods and forced to rely on meager handouts at government agencies. Worse still, whole bands contracted smallpox, measles and other European diseases, and warriors, unable to feed their families or hunt, became addicted to alcohol.

Raven sought to restrain their people from attacking settlements, treaties were repeatedly broken by settlers. Indians had no recourse but to fight back, flee, or accept what was offered.

Tragedy followed tragedy. On November 29, 1864, trigger-happy Colorado volunteers led by Colonel John Chivington took matters into their own hands and slaughtered 137 innocent women, children and old men at Sand Creek, near the Arkansas River. Among them were Chiefs Left Hand and White Antelope. Indian counterattacks lasted two years, then, in 1867, huge losses led Kiowa, Cheyenne, Southern Arapaho and Comanche leaders to sign the Medicine Lodge

Plains people grew increasingly desperate, and many young men turned to raiding white settlements in order to feed their starving families. The government took a hardline policy of rounding up tribes by whatever means necessary and placing them on reservations. Hunters were expected to take up farming, live with former enemies, own property, and give up their language and culture. For the nomadic tribes of Colorado, it was a disaster. As leaders such as Ouray, Black Kettle, White Antelope and Little

LEFT: mounted hunters pursue bison in Charles M. Russell's *The Buffalo Hunt No. 39*.
ABOVE: the Sand Creek Massacre.

Treaty confining their tribes to reservations in the Oklahoma and Kansas territories.

Many tribal members refused to go, but resistance proved futile. In November 1868, the Cheyenne leader Black Kettle, who had miraculously survived the massacre at Sand Creek, was shot down in cold blood by General George Armstrong Custer at Washita River, Oklahoma. Ten years later, the Northern Arapaho were moved to the Shoshone Reservation near the Wind River in Wyoming. The only tribe left in Colorado were the Utes, whose leaders – Ouray, Severo and Ignacio – were left with no choice but to breach the growing divide between their people and gold-hungry whites flooding into Colorado. ❑

BREAKING GROUND

*Spaniards and other strangers barged right in, reconfiguring
the social landscape and rewriting a whole region's history*

Colorado has plenty of spacious skies and purple mountain majesties but not a whole lot of modern history, especially as compared to a place like neighboring New Mexico. The latter was an important offshoot of New Spain, whereas Colorado was long considered remote and unpromising. Not until after the mid-19th century, when precious metals were mined and fortunes started piling up, did much development take place.

As for the native cliff dwellers, they had largely abandoned the place for a long time, leaving only nomadic Indian hunters to roam a land that in earlier times had been home to vibrant Pueblo civilizations. Minimal, too, was the Spanish presence. Twenty years or so after turning Mexico into an Iberian offshoot, conquistadors ventured north in pursuit of supposedly fabulous riches, blazing a trail that led to important centers like Santa Fe and Taos but little in the way of settlements in the land beyond.

Most famous of those Spanish pioneers was Francisco Vásquez de Coronado. Setting out with a large force in 1540 to find the supposedly fabulous "Seven Cities of Cíbola," he headed up the Rio Grande into New Mexico, found only some rather modest Pueblo communities, and returned to Mexico City two years later. In the process, he is thought to have traipsed across some part of southeastern Colorado, as perhaps the first of the European visitors.

Coronado's explorers broke a lot of ground, beheld wondrous sights, and coined some place-names, including their descriptive for the reddish or ruddy look of a great river they encountered – "colorado." But little subsequent effort was made to plant settlements in the fertile lands of the Colorado-to-be. Perhaps the expense was forbidding for New Spain's cost-conscious bureaucrats. Or perhaps it was a fear of tangling with the fiercely independent Indians to the north, including Utes and Comanches who would not have been well-disposed to hewing wood, carrying water or taking up farming on anyone's behalf.

Nonetheless, Spain did authorize expeditions from Mexico City in the course of the 17th century, leading to the discovery of various Indian settlements. Traders gradually ventured north, and by 1700 goods were being exchanged at

settlements near present-day La Junta, a place on the Arkansas River close to the site where in later years Bent's Fort would become a landmark exchange place on the famous Santa Fe Trail for fur trappers, traders and mountain men.

The French connection

Others besides Spaniards showed up, chiefly French and English and, ultimately, the newly independent Americans representing a dynamic young republic which, as the 19th century dawned, began spreading across the continent.

Early on, Spain and France dueled for proprietorship over the region west of the Mississippi River that came to be known as the Great Plains.

LEFT: a Cheyenne man, c.1910; the Cheyenne roamed the plains of eastern Colorado until the 1860s.
RIGHT: Stephen H. Long, leader of an 1820 expedition.

This was a lot of land with a lot of natural resources, and it was claimed for France by the explorer La Salle in 1682. After leading a party of about 50 men downriver to the Gulf of Mexico, he grandly declared the entire territory between the Alleghenies and the Rockies to be the property of Louis XIV. Hence the name Louisiana.

A similar claim was made on Spain's behalf in 1706 by Juan de Uribarri, who frequently chased across the land after Indian slaves fleeing their New Mexican masters. Becoming concerned about possible French intrusion via the Mississippi River, Uribarri declared the region to be part of the Spanish realm.

present-day eastern Colorado and Nebraska, was caught up in an ambush by Pawnee Indians at the Platte River in Nebraska. Villasur and nearly his entire force were wiped out.

In the 18th century, French *voyageurs* roamed around a good part of the land that later was involved in the history-making Louisiana Purchase. The first known French explorers in the region were the Mallet brothers, Pierre and Paul, in 1739–41. Their expedition went from Canada to Santa Fe, where they spent nearly a year and wound up giving away all their goods, an action which has caused historians to suspect that perhaps what the Mallets were really

Spanish authorities became obsessed with voyageurs. These were the trappers, often the offspring of French males and Indian females, who hunted beaver and other fur-bearing animals, conveying the pelts to market on canoe voyages. Fur was big business. Hats made of beaver fur were long popular in Europe, and the trade played a major role in opening up the American West to settlement.

So the turf was declared off-limits by Spanish overlords, quick to head off anything that smacked of trading activity. One such Spanish reaction in 1720 had disastrous results. An expedition under Pedro de Villasur, checking on reports that French settlers were infiltrating

interested in was sniffing out gold and silver mining deposits.

More of the Frenchmen came in the years ahead, traveling a route that became the storied Santa Fe Trail. But overall their influence was minimal, and when the Seven Years War was terminated in 1763, France was compelled to bow out of the American picture. The French ceded to Britain and Spain, respectively, territories east and west of the Mississippi River.

France did get back the western land, which included Colorado, in an 1801 agreement with Spain. But the restoration was short-lived. Two years later, the Louisiana Purchase brought an end to French designs on North America.

The searchers

Colorado's awesome landscape was spotlighted with great effect by a couple of Franciscan friars turned explorers after a memorable if not foolhardy journey in 1776. The intrepid padres were Francisco Dominguez and Silvestre Escalante, accompanied by eight friends. Going forth from Santa Fe in search of a shorter route between the missions of New Mexico and California, they roamed southwest Colorado and later described in print such vividly named places as the Sangre de Cristo (Blood of Christ) mountains and El Rio de Las Animas Perdidas en Purgatorio (River of Lost Souls in Purgatory).

In Colorado also, three years later, a Comanche warrior named Cuerno Verde was brought down in a bloody battle in the Greenhorn Mountains south of the Arkansas River by an armed force headed by New Mexico's governor, Juan Bautista de Anza. Cuerno Verde and his fighters were pursued northward out of the San Luis Valley onto the plains below Pikes Peak before they were cornered, many dying along with their chief.

Spain's claim to the Colorado territory was reinforced through such military expeditions and other activities, including searches for precious metals. Mining was carried out successfully elsewhere in the New World, so Spanish authorities were always alert to evidence of any precious metals in the greater New Mexico territory.

An early effort at prospecting was made in 1765 when a group headed by Juan Maria de Rivera came north from Santa Fe to search for gold in the San Juan and Sangre de Cristo mountains. Although unsuccessful, they were the first known outsiders to explore what became known as the Gunnison River.

Westward ho!

Colorado's story takes a great leap forward with the Louisiana Purchase. That big deal added most of what is now eastern Colorado to the fledgling nation, although exactly where the boundary lay between the Spanish and American realms was left in doubt – was it the Arkansas River or was it the more southern Red River? It would take until 1850 for Colorado's physical shape to be configured once and for all.

One of those who went forth to chart the

West's topography was a young army officer named Zebulon Montgomery Pike. In 1806 he headed a 22-man expedition instructed to gather information on the source of the Arkansas and Red Rivers and on Spanish settlements in New Mexico. Traveling up the Arkansas to the vicinity of present-day Pueblo, the explorers spotted in the distance a tall snow-covered mountain later to be named Pikes Peak. It took them two weeks to reach the mountain, and when they tried to climb to the top, Pike and his men were unsuccessful.

Arrested by a Spanish military force, the Americans were interrogated and held for a time at Santa Fe and Chihuahua, Mexico. Pike was freed

in July 1807. He died five years later in the War of 1812 in Canada. Another expedition led by a U.S. Army officer, Major Stephen H. Long, went forth in 1820, this time at the bidding of President James Monroe. The instructions were to explore the southwest boundary of the territory acquired in the Louisiana Purchase. Long's group entered Colorado via the South Platte River and explored much of the Rockies' eastern flank.

This time, Pikes Peak was successfully scaled. The man who did it was Dr. Edwin James, the Long expedition's botanist and historian. Long named it James Peak, but hunters and trappers persisted in calling it Pikes Peak and that name stuck.

LEFT: John C. Frémont planting an American flag in the Rocky Mountains in an 1856 campaign illustration.
RIGHT: Kit Carson served as Frémont's guide.

Climb every mountain

The true western pioneers were the trailblazers who operated as scouts and trappers. Known as plainsmen and even more famously as mountain men, these rugged individualists pushed deep into the wilderness combing for beaver and other fur-bearing animals and becoming the stuff of frontier legend.

Their names are well-known, among them Jim Bridger and Jim Beckwourth and Jim Baker, Tom "Broken Hand" Fitzpatrick and "Uncle Dick" Wootton, and the legendary Kit Carson, that all-purpose scout, fighter and Indian expert. Traversing a wide expanse, these

that an enduring peace agreement was hammered out at an extraordinary meeting of Arapaho, Kiowa, Cheyenne and Comanche chiefs.

Another busy trading post was Fort Vasquez, built for the Rocky Mountain Fur Company on the South Platte River north of what became the city of Denver. It was frequented by American trappers and hunters as well as members of Cheyenne and Arapaho tribes. In 1842, however, it was looted by Indian raiders. After the demand for beaver dried up, trading posts were generally abandoned. To protect isolated frontier settlements and trading routes, the federal government put up a string of military forts.

prototypical free-traders forded streams and climbed mountains for furs and other items and in the process became intimate with the native inhabitants of the Colorado Rockies. Prices for beaver pelts soared in the 1820s and remained high until supplies diminished and the market collapsed in the late 1830s.

Carson was a familiar figure at one of the most famous of the western trading posts: Bent's Fort. The first Anglo settlement in what became Colorado, it was built in 1832 by William Bent, his three brothers and their partner Ceran St. Vrain near the present-day city of La Junta. Indians, too, traded at this early mercantile establishment, and it was here in 1840

Kit Carson lived for many years in Colorado. Having commanded a Union force in the Civil War, he was named to head Fort Garland, in the San Luis Valley, in 1866. He died two years later at nearby Fort Lyon. One of the many personalities he served as guide was another public figure whose name ranks high in western annals, the flamboyant John Charles Frémont.

Ah, wilderness!

Frémont's enduring contribution was to stimulate public interest in the American West. He was a native Easterner, like so many who figure prominently in the Colorado story. Starting in 1842 as a lieutenant with the U.S. Army, he